VACATIONS, PARTIES, PEOPLE, AND PLACES

Alan Snow

Derrydale Books
New York

On Vacation

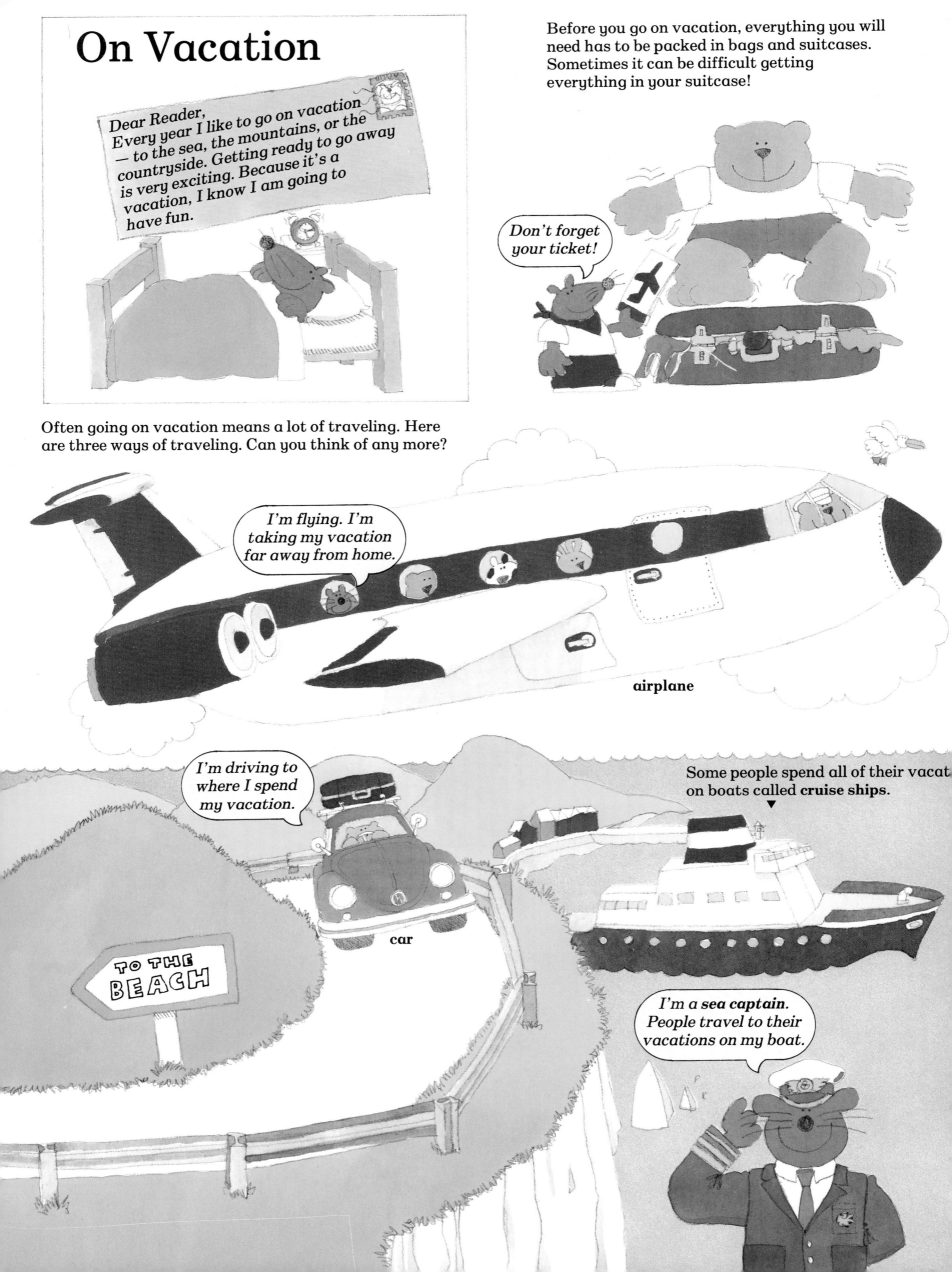

Dear Reader,
Every year I like to go on vacation — to the sea, the mountains, or the countryside. Getting ready to go away is very exciting. Because it's a vacation, I know I am going to have fun.

Before you go on vacation, everything you will need has to be packed in bags and suitcases. Sometimes it can be difficult getting everything in your suitcase!

Don't forget your ticket!

Often going on vacation means a lot of traveling. Here are three ways of traveling. Can you think of any more?

I'm flying. I'm taking my vacation far away from home.

airplane

I'm driving to where I spend my vacation.

car

TO THE BEACH

Some people spend all of their vacat on boats called **cruise ships**.

I'm a **sea captain**. People travel to their vacations on my boat.

By the Seashore

Look at this seashore scene. Can you see someone swimming, someone sailing, and someone fishing? What other things are these vacationers doing?

seagull

kite

telescope

lighthouse

fisherman

rowboat

crab

fish net

diver

sailboat

Exploring rock pools.

When the tide goes out you can find little pools left behind. All sorts of creatures live in them. Here are some you might find if you went to the seashore.

ice cream stand

cave

umbrella

cliff

beach

bucket and shovel

seashell

beach ball

beach chair

toy boat

seaweed

starfish

raft

swimmer

Going to Town

Towns are busy places. People go there to shop, or to work, or just to look around. It's fun going to town, but watch out for all the cars and trucks.

This is a **bicycle shop**. It sells bicycles and repairs them when they are broken.

This is a **restaurant**, where you can buy a meal to eat.

window washer

newspaper stand

street cleaner

Visiting the Dentist

A dentist's job is very special as he or she cares for your teeth. Your teeth should last all of your life, and the dentist takes great care to make sure they do. You visit the dentist to have your teeth and gums checked to make sure they are clean and healthy. If you do get a toothache, the dentist can make it better. You can help your dentist by brushing and flossing three times a day, and by not eating too many sweets!

Brushing teeth regularly with a **toothbrush** and **toothpaste** helps prevent tooth decay.

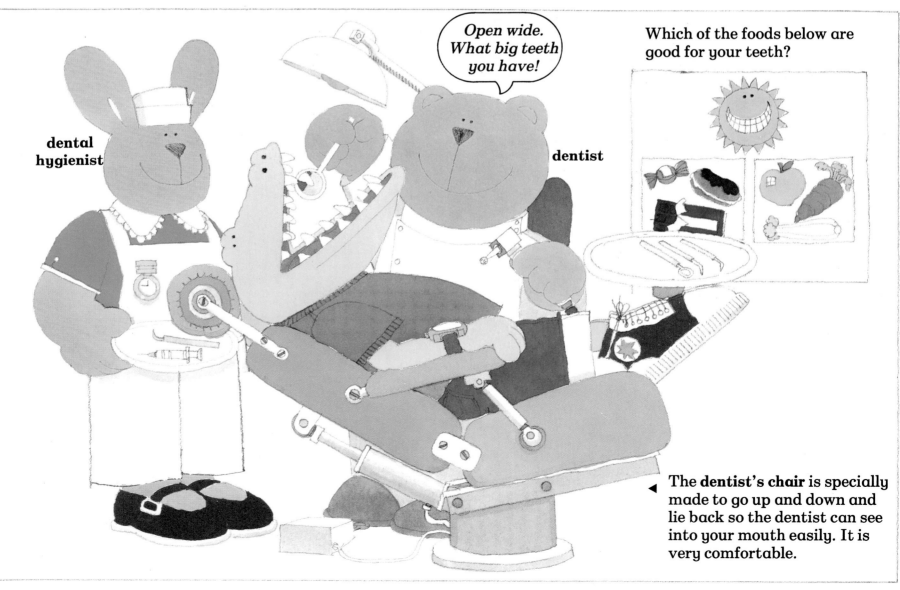

dental hygienist

Open wide. What big teeth you have!

dentist

Which of the foods below are good for your teeth?

◄ The **dentist's chair** is specially made to go up and down and lie back so the dentist can see into your mouth easily. It is very comfortable.

Visiting the Doctor

If you are sick or hurt you might go and visit a doctor. Sometimes he or she will come and visit you at home. A doctor will ask you questions and look at you very carefully to find out what's wrong. The doctor will decide how to make you well again, which might mean taking some medicine — it might not taste very good but it will make you feel better!

If you break a leg you wear a **plaster cast** to keep it still until it heals.

If you hurt your arm you might wear a **sling** to give it support. ▶

Bandages are for covering cuts and scrapes.

Medicine helps you to get better. Never take any medicine unless a grown-up tells you to. ▶

eye-test chart

stethoscope

medicine cabinet

A **nurse** looks after people who are sick and helps the doctor make them better.

I feel better already!

thermometer

doctor

patient

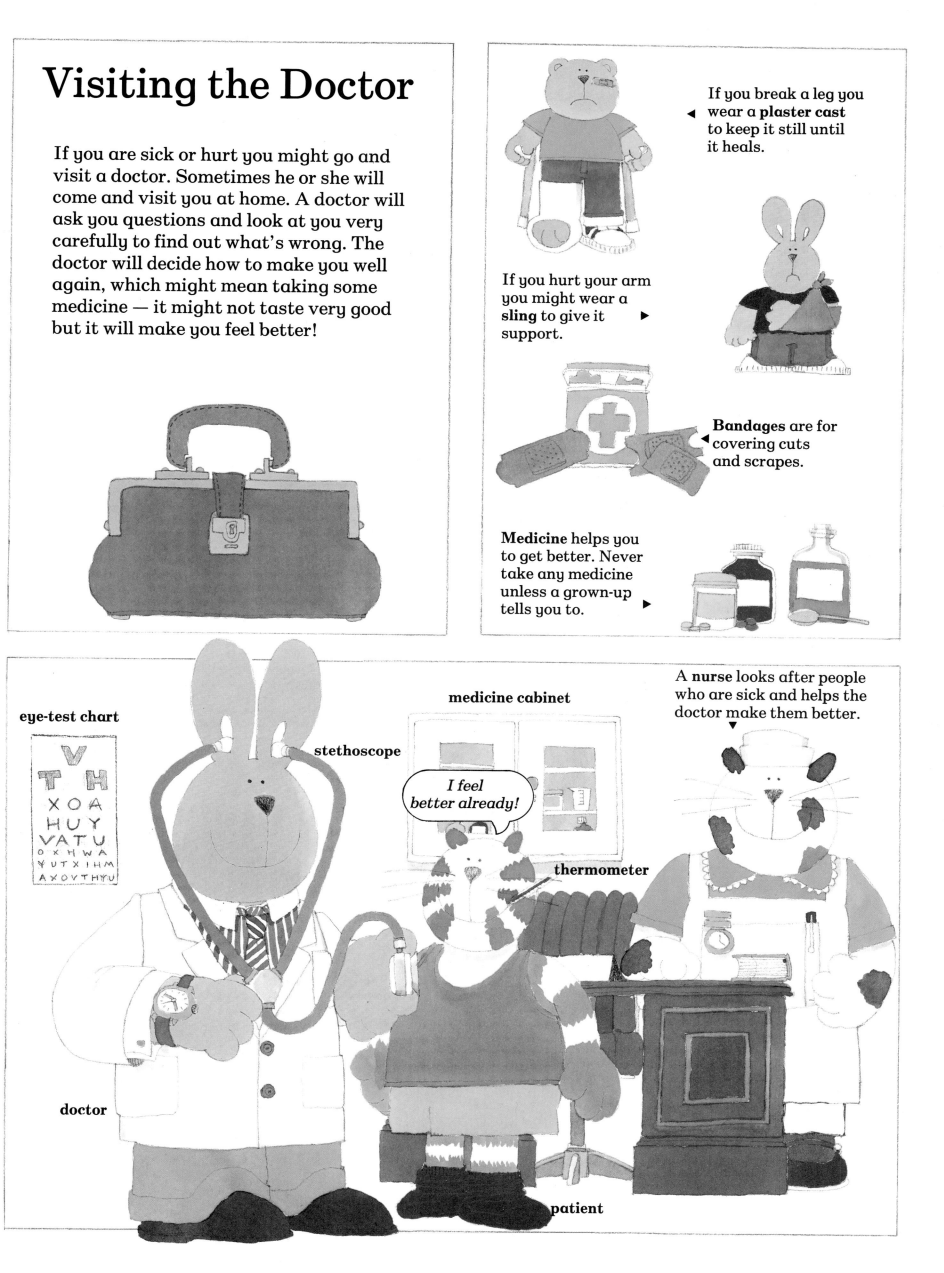

At the Supermarket

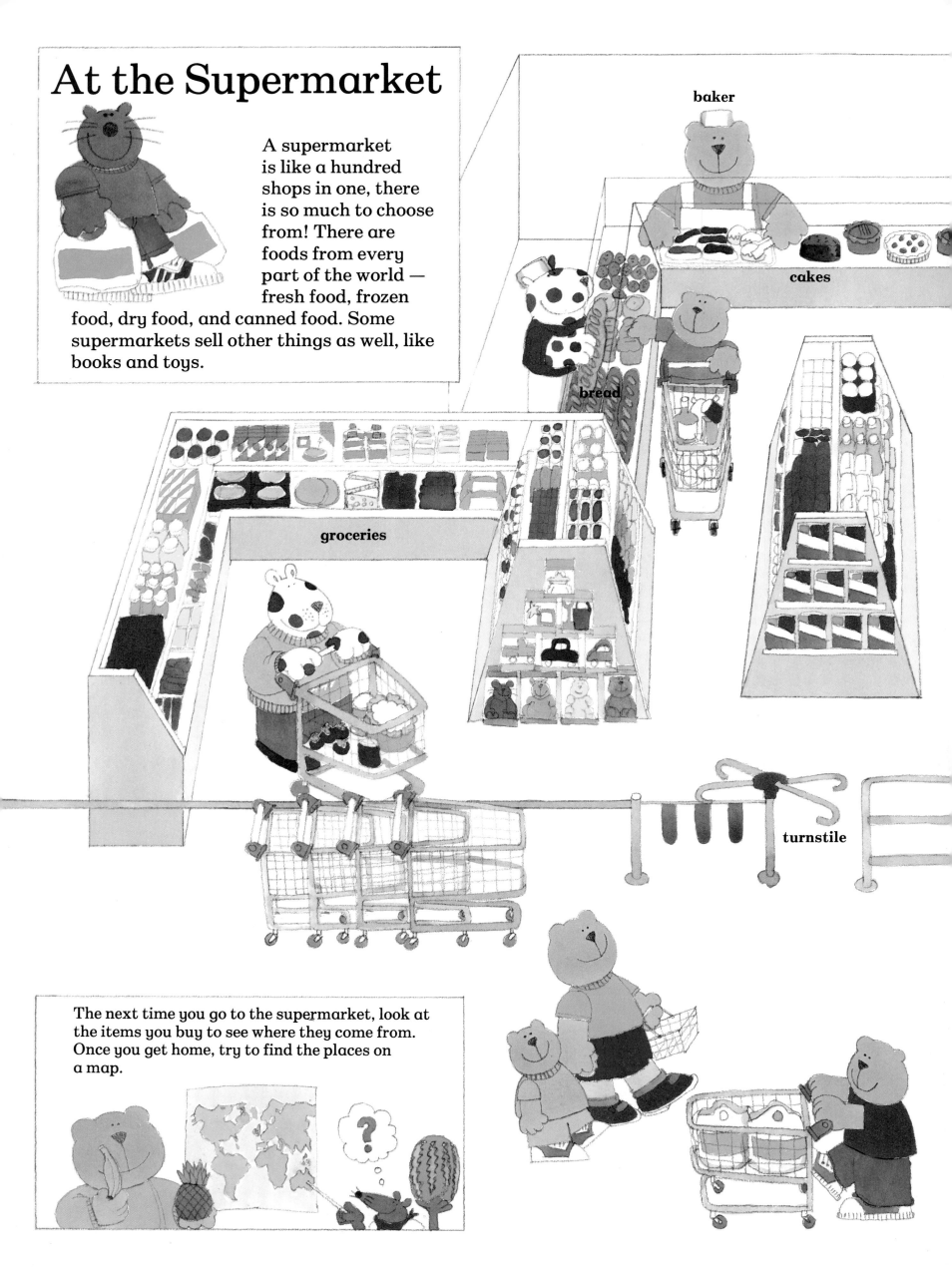

A supermarket is like a hundred shops in one, there is so much to choose from! There are foods from every part of the world — fresh food, frozen food, dry food, and canned food. Some supermarkets sell other things as well, like books and toys.

baker

cakes

bread

groceries

turnstile

The next time you go to the supermarket, look at the items you buy to see where they come from. Once you get home, try to find the places on a map.

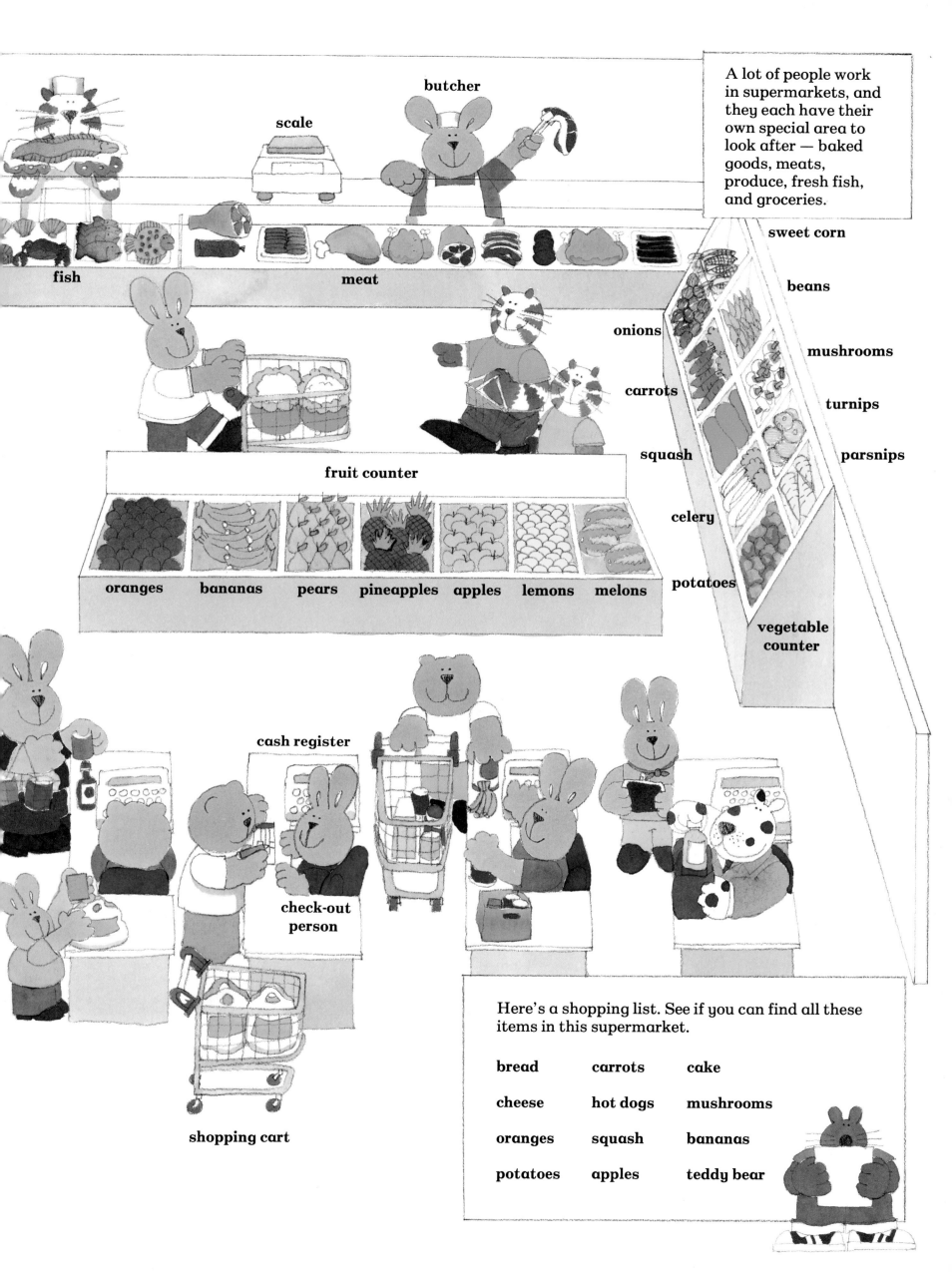

butcher

scale

sweet corn

beans

mushrooms

onions

turnips

carrots

parsnips

squash

fish

meat

celery

fruit counter

potatoes

vegetable
counter

oranges   bananas   pears   pineapples   apples   lemons   melons

A lot of people work in supermarkets, and they each have their own special area to look after — baked goods, meats, produce, fresh fish, and groceries.

cash register

check-out
person

shopping cart

Here's a shopping list. See if you can find all these items in this supermarket.

bread	carrots	cake
cheese	hot dogs	mushrooms
oranges	squash	bananas
potatoes	apples	teddy bear

Going Swimming

Going to the swimming pool is fun, once you have learned how to swim. There are many different swimming strokes. Here are some you can try.

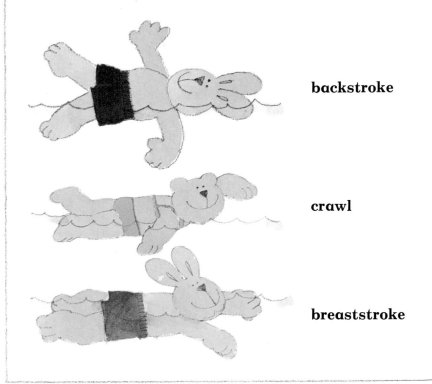

backstroke

crawl

breaststroke

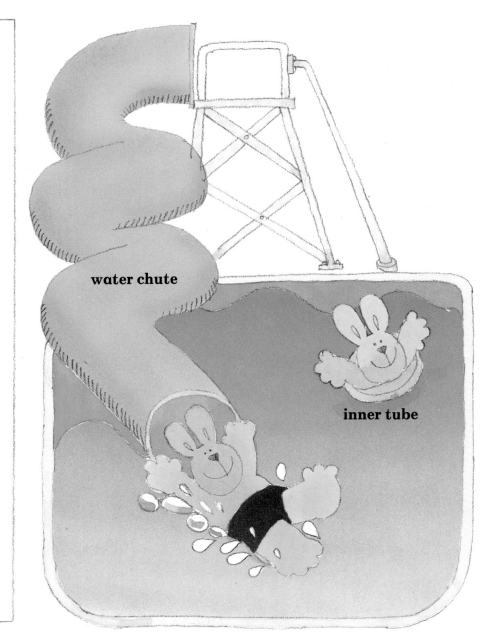

water chute

inner tube

Here are some swimming aids:
1. **Goggles** to keep water out of your eyes.
2. **Water wings** to stop you from sinking.
3. **Flippers** to make you go fast.
4. **Nose clip** to stop water from going up your nose.
5. **Inner tube** to help you float.

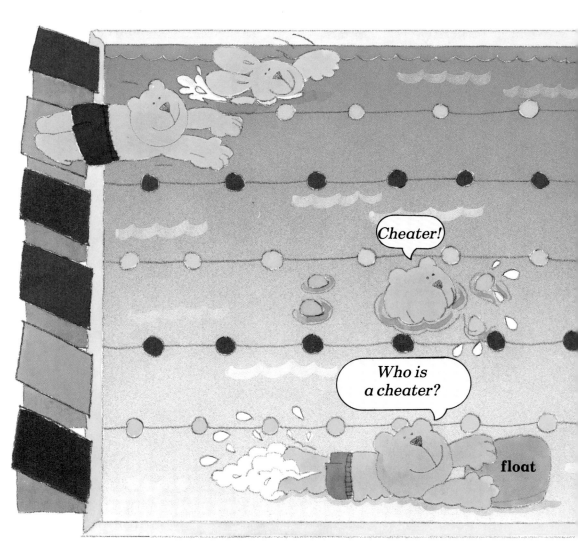

Athletics

Welcome to the Athletics Stadium. There are a lot of different sports to watch. Look at all the athletes — see how fast they can run, see how high they can jump, see how far they can throw!

Wait for me!

spectators

sprinter

marathon runner

An **electronic eye** times the athletes.

The longest race is the **marathon**. It is over 26 miles long.

electronic scoreboard

crossbar

The **running track** is 400-meters long and oval shaped. The best tracks are made of rubber.

high jumper

Pole vaulters use a long springy pole to launch themselves into the air and over the crossbar. ▶

pole

landing mat

In the **high jump** the crossbar is moved up and up to see who can jump the highest.

track

Long jumpers need to run first to help them jump farther. ▶

long jumper

This **landing mat** stops jumpers from hurting themselves when they land.

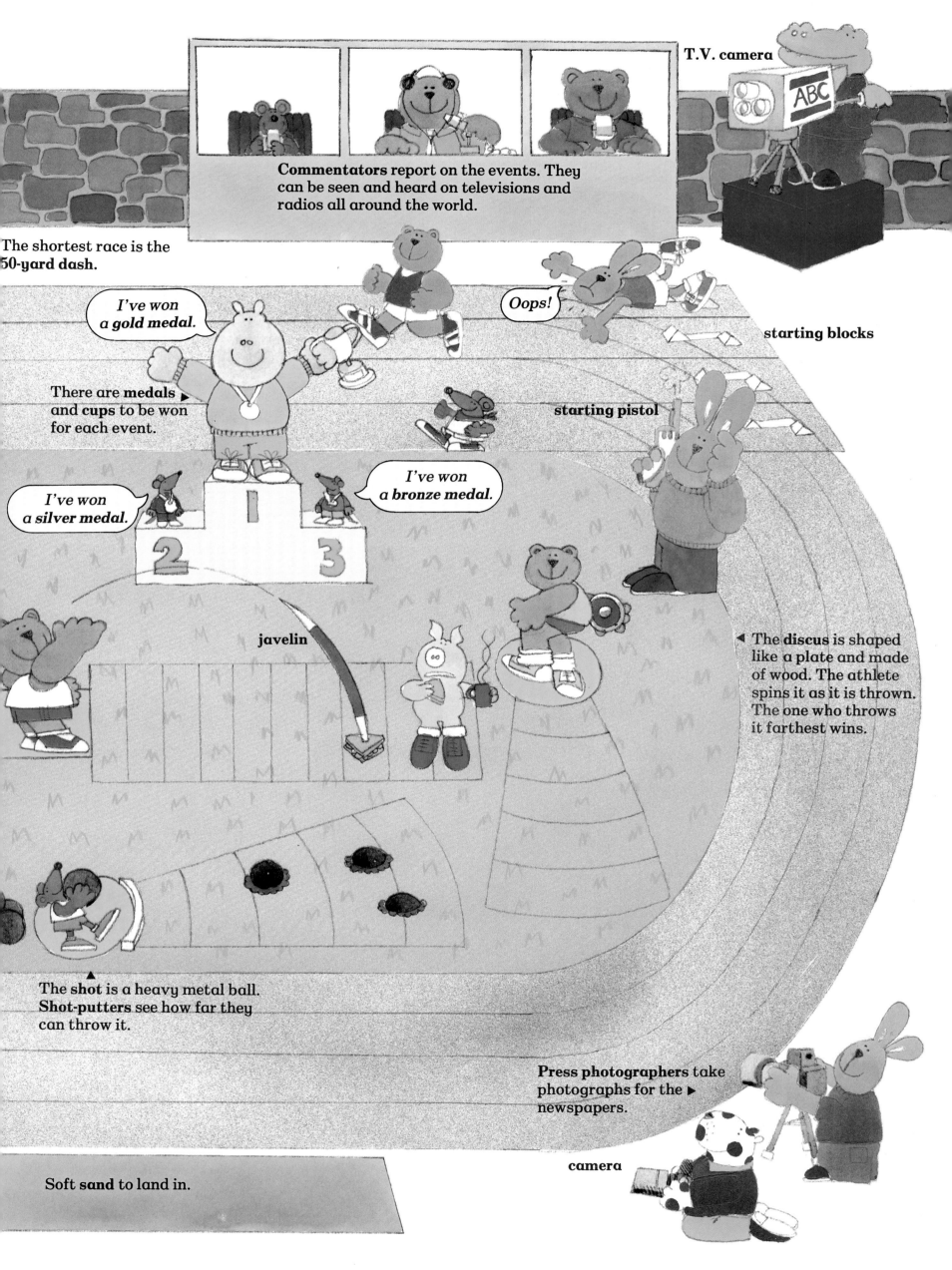

At the Museum

A museum is a place where a collection of beautiful, rare, or very old things is kept. People, who are specialists, travel all over the world looking for objects to add to the museum's collection.

The Aztecs from Central America built temples like these.

The Egyptians buried their kings and their treasures in pyramids like these.

How did people live hundreds of years ago? Archeologists, who discover old cities, temples, and towns help us find out. You can see what they discovered in museums.

Here are some things you might see in a museum.

galleon model

early airplane

pottery

Egyptian mummy

antique car

paintings

model village

dinosaur

steam engine

sword and shield

At the Zoo

You don't have to travel around the world to see elephants or giraffes. You can see them at the zoo. All kinds of animals are kept in zoos so we can learn more about them — and enjoy visiting them too.

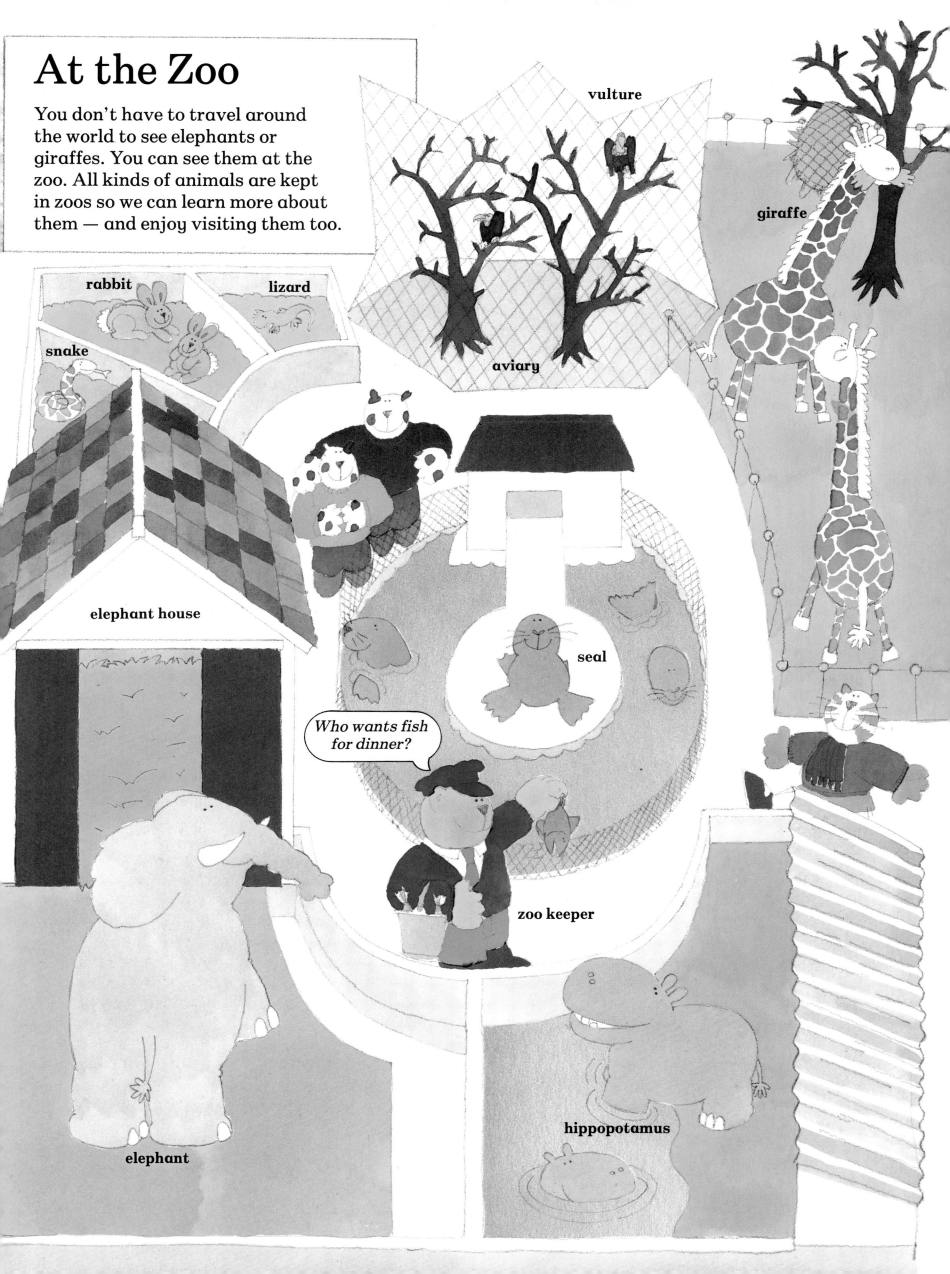

vulture

giraffe

rabbit

lizard

snake

aviary

elephant house

seal

Who wants fish for dinner?

zoo keeper

elephant

hippopotamus

Going to School

Every morning the **school bus** picks up many of the children and takes them to school.

When you first go to school, you may not know anyone and it all seems very strange. But soon, when you make friends, and begin learning so many new things, you find out that school is fun. Here are some children at school. Of all the things they are doing, which do you like doing best?

Before classes begin there is time to play on the playground.

ball

basketball net

doll

book bag

toy car

playground

The children in kindergarten play most of the day. Their teacher helps them to paint, draw, and make things.

The older children learn to read and write.

Party Time

At parties there are games to play, friends to play with, and delicious food to eat. Sometimes there are presents and prizes to win.

When you go to a party it's nice to wear your best clothes. You might take a present if it's a birthday party. Remember your manners — always say please and thank you.

Happy birthday to you, Happy birthday to you!

There are always games to play. What's your favorite party game?

Let's play this tape and dance!

cassette player

presents

television